The Pocket Book of Frame Games

The Pocket Book of FRAME GAMES

Terry Stickels

GLOUCESTER, MASSACHUSETTS

First published in the USA in 2006 by
Fair Winds Press, a member of
Quayside Publishing Group
33 Commercial Street
Gloucester, MA 01930

10 09 08 07 06 2 3 4 5

ISBN 1-59233-195-5

Cover design by Scott Kim
Book design & illustration by Scott Kim

Printed and bound in Canada

Foreword

Terry Stickels has been a staple in the puzzling community for years now, and his puzzles have universal appeal to both experts and amateurs alike. With so many copycats on the market, it's always refreshing when one of the masters releases a new book.

His latest book, *The Pocket Book of Frame Games*, is full of Terry's trademark puzzle, the frame game. Always a crowd-pleaser, frame games challenge you to come up with a well-known saying, person, place, or thing. Many offer visual puns with a combination of writing and images. Other books may try to duplicate the success of Terry's frame games, but his are the best around, and nobody gets as creative as Terry when it comes to stumping puzzlers with unique and refreshing puzzles.

Science now tells us that exercising our brains is just as important as exercising our bodies. Frame games are a perfect way to test your mental flexibility and keep your brain sharp.

Over the years, I've become a great fan of Terry and the way he makes me think. This book is superb. If you like puzzles, do yourself a favor and buy this book!

—*Nathan Haselbauer*
President and Founder
International High IQ Society

Answer on page 8

Answer on page 9

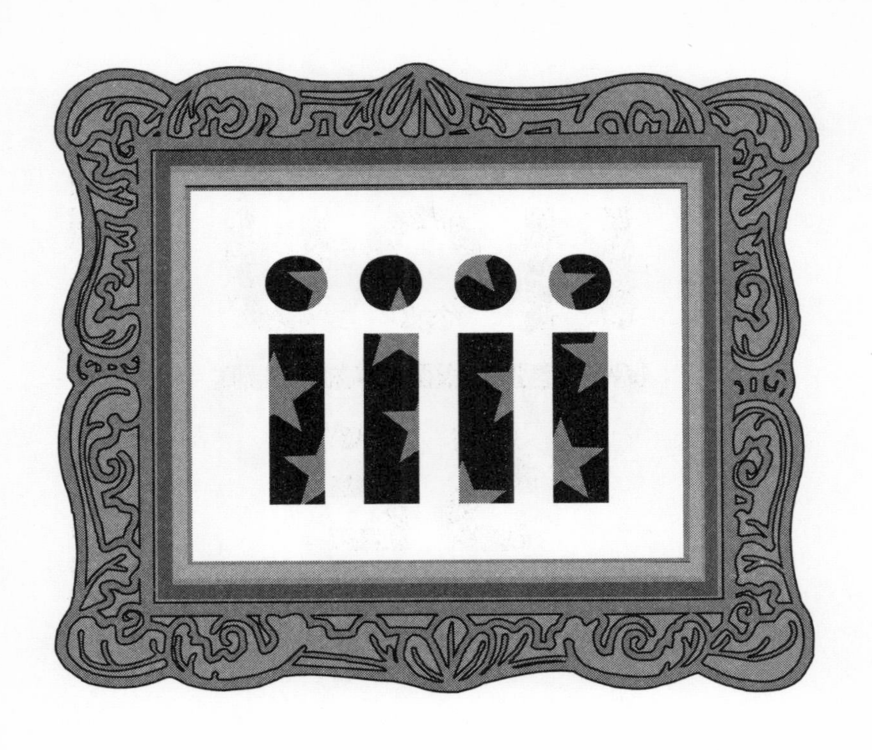

Answer to 6: fading fast

9

Answer to 7: running around in circles

Answer to 8: stars in your eyes

Answer to 9: a house divided

Answer to 10: eavesdropping

Answer to 13: expanding universe

Answer to 12: foul language

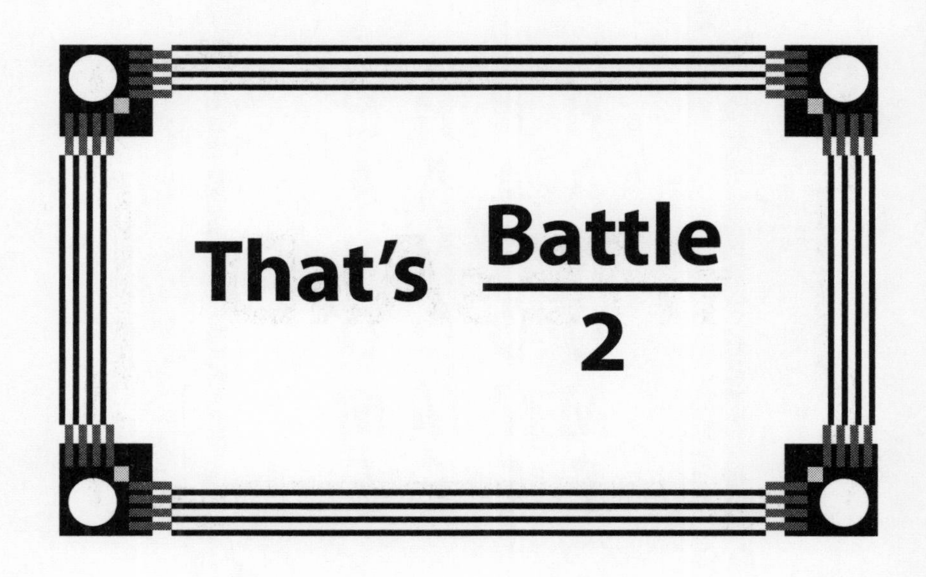

Answer to13: first and foremost

Answer to 14: head in the sand

Answer to 15: that's half the battle

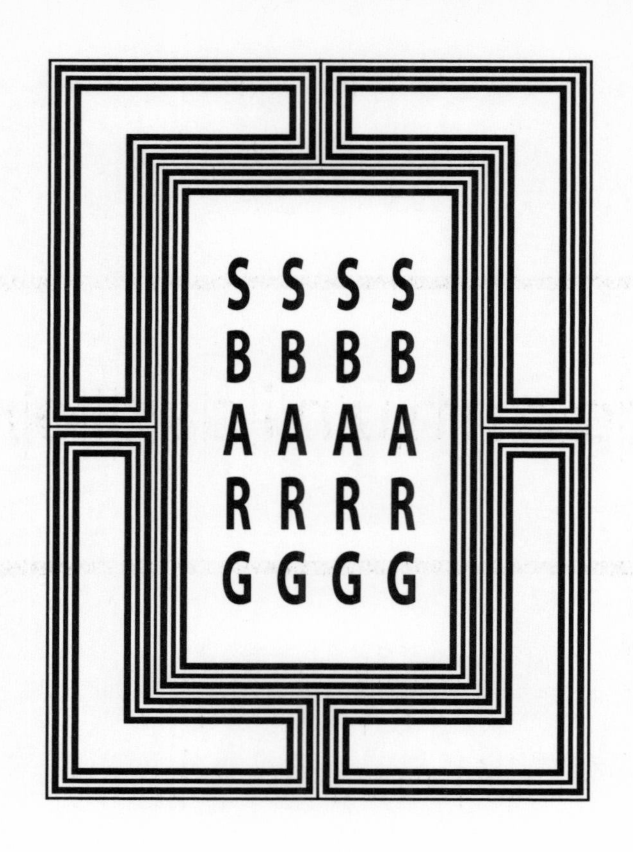

Answer to 16: hand me downs

Answer to 17: angel eyes

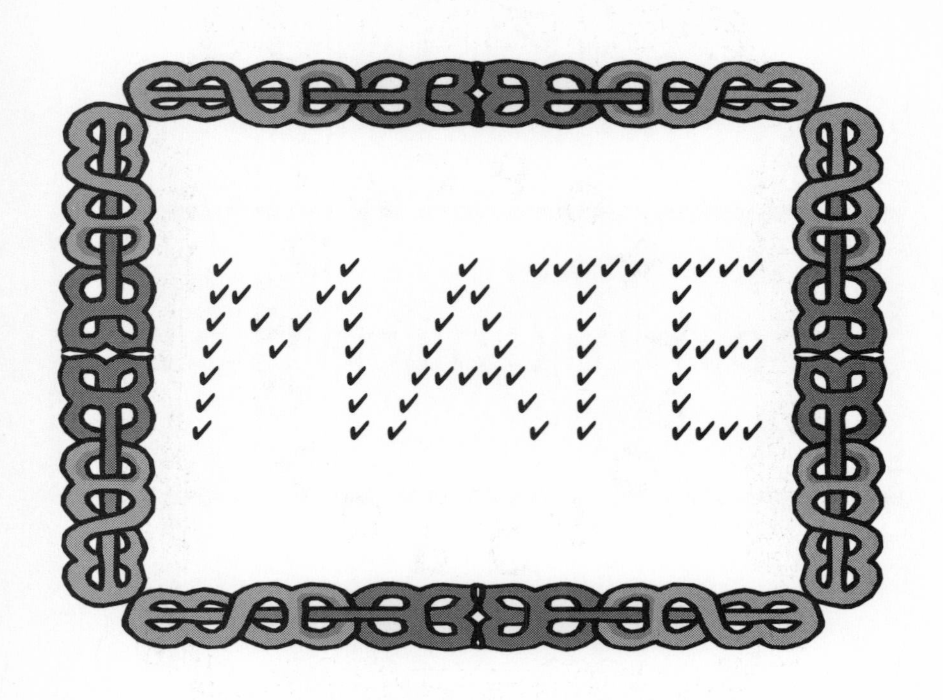

Answer to 18: up for grabs

Answer to 19: lines of communication

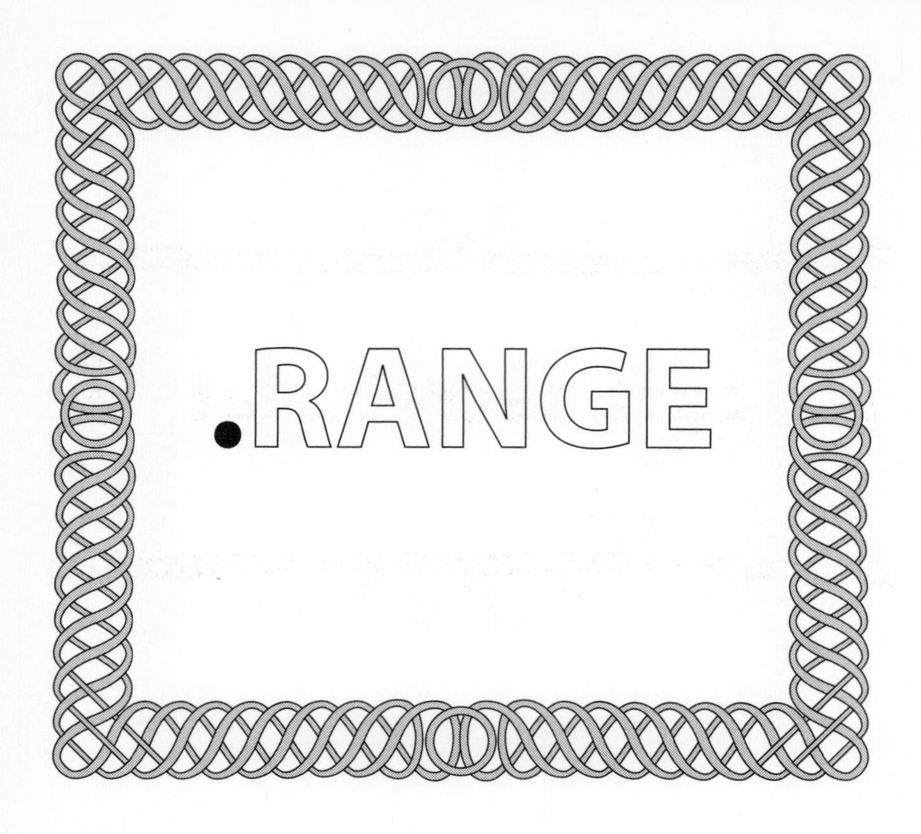

Answer to 20: checkmate

Answer to 21: crop rotation

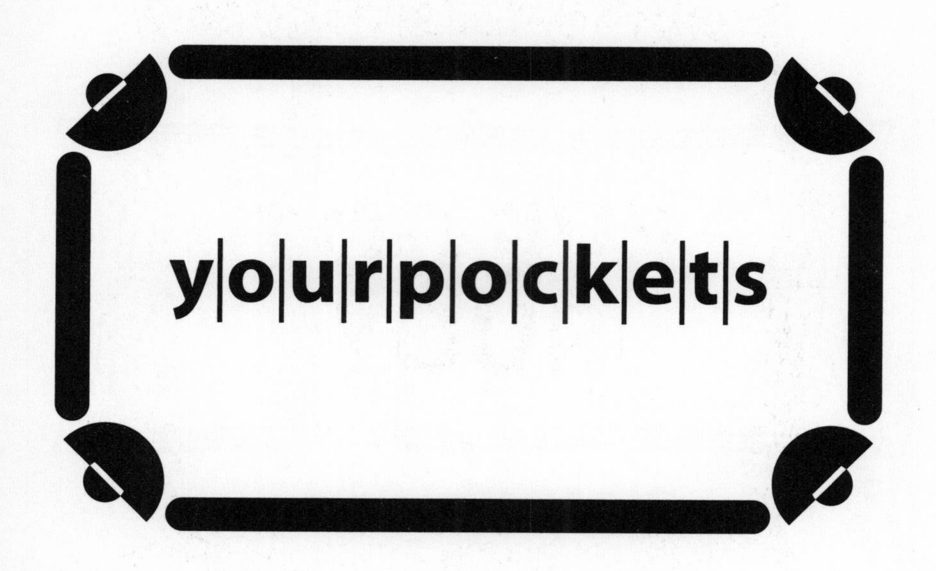

Answer to 22: point blank range

Answer to 23: putting the cart before the horse

DAY

Answer to 24: lining your pockets

Answer to 25: I've got your back

Answer to 26: day in, day out

Answer to 27: working up a sweat

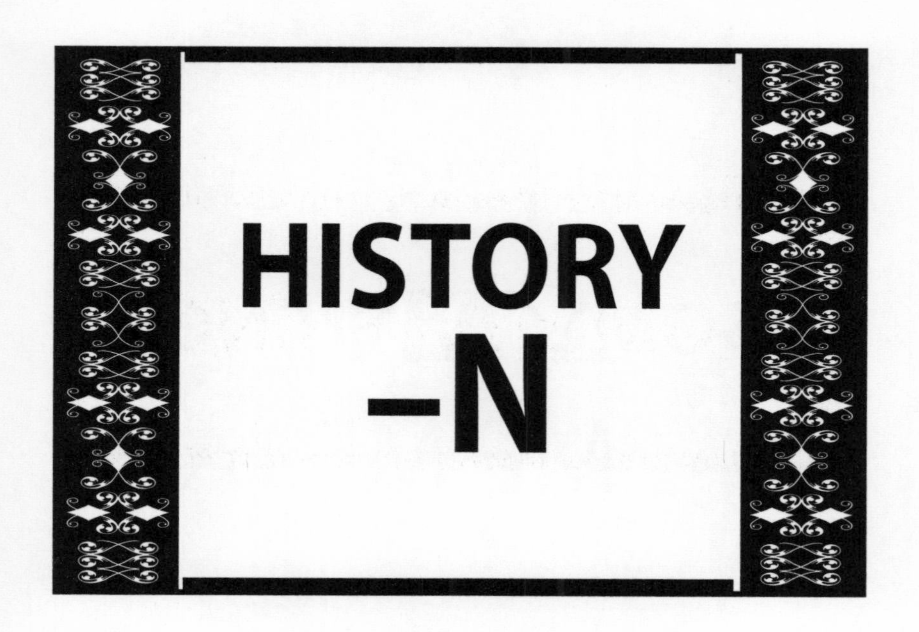

Answer to 28: bride to be

SOME**IM**THING

Answer to 29: it's Greek to me

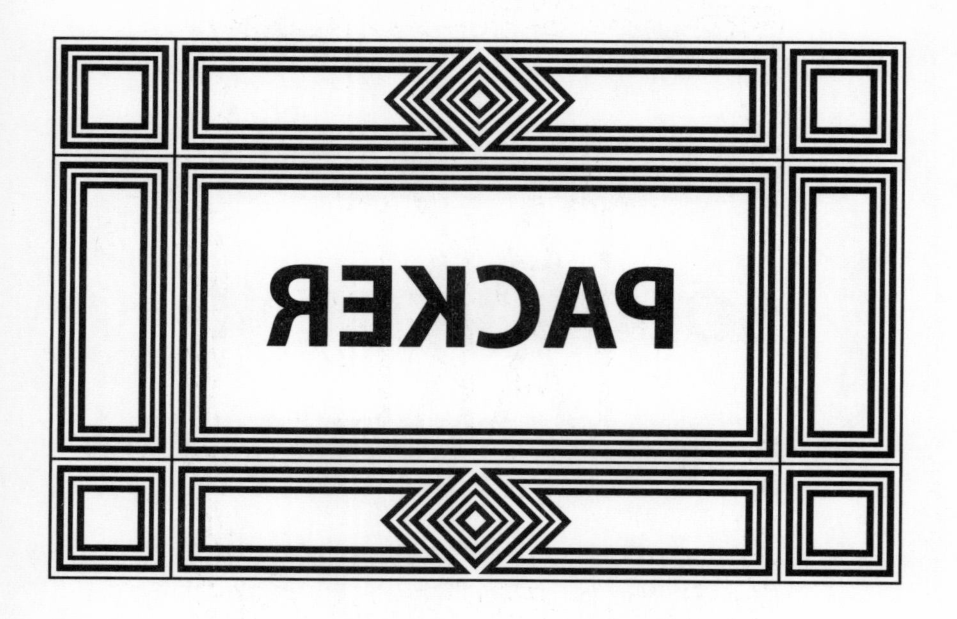

Answer to 30: history lesson

Answer to 31: I'm in the middle of something

Answer to 32: backpacker

Answer to 33: doubletake

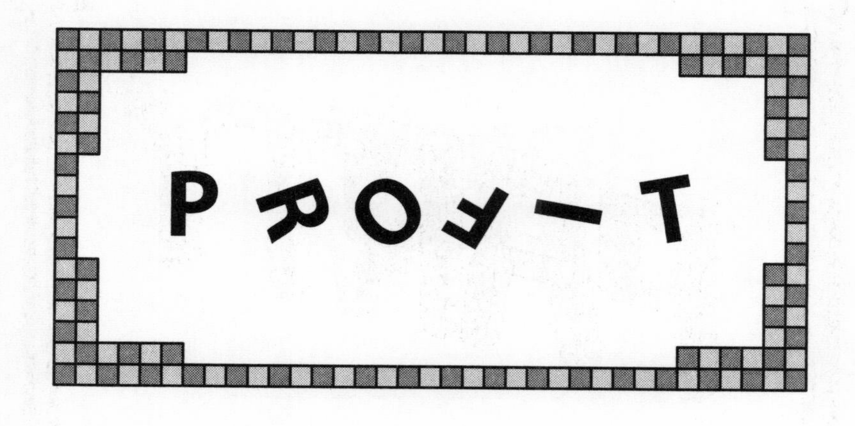

Answer to 34: strength in numbers

Answer to 35: on further review

Answer to 36: turning a profit

Answer to 37: block party

Answer to 38: the land down under

Answer to 39: don't beat around the bush

Answer to 40: dividing the spoils

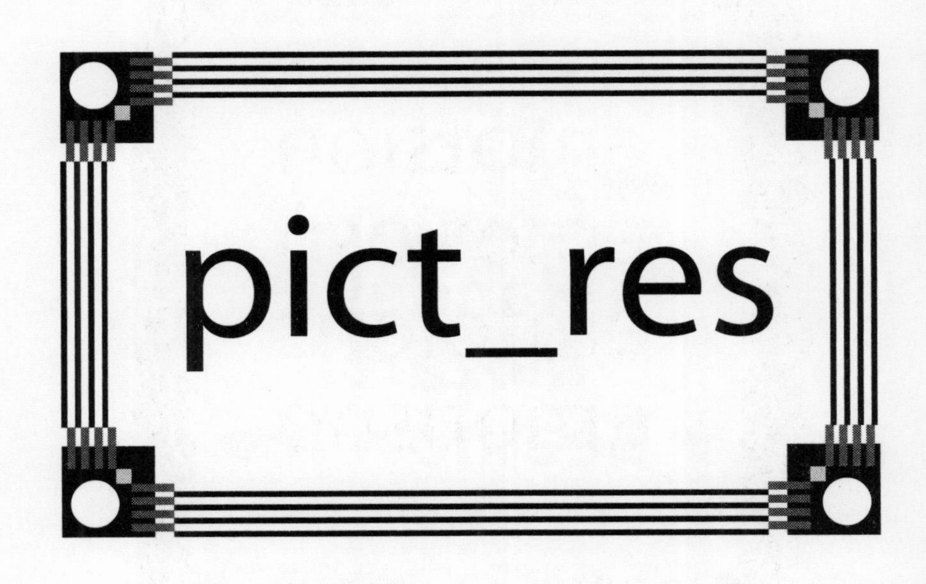

Answer to 41: choke up on the bat

Answer to 42: mixed emotions

Answer to 43: you ought to be in pictures

Answer to 44: Beethoven's Fifth

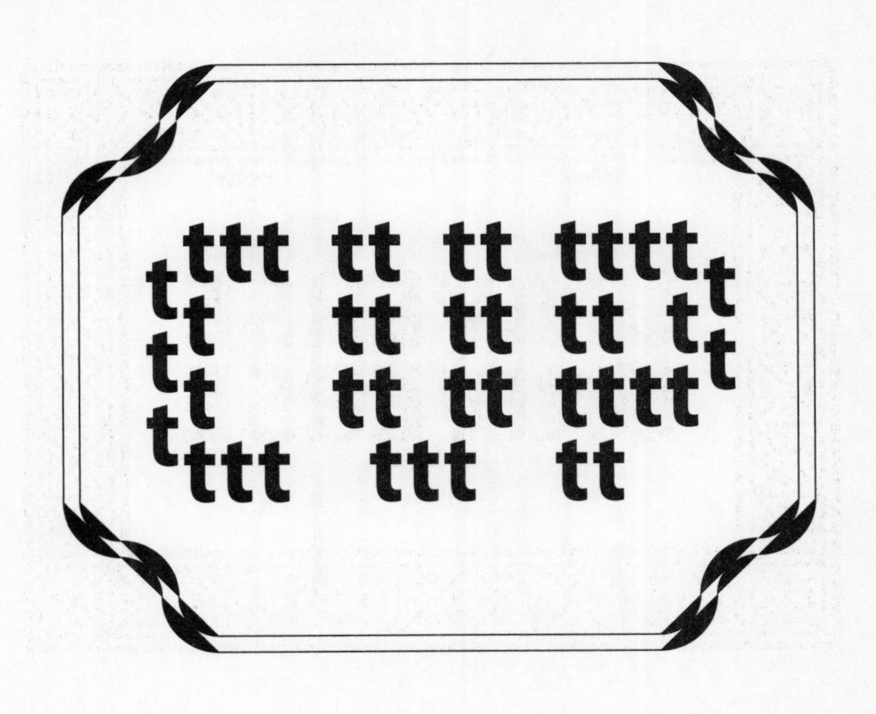

Answer to 45: rub the wrong way

Answer to 46: parallel universes

Answer to 47: cup of tea (or teacup)

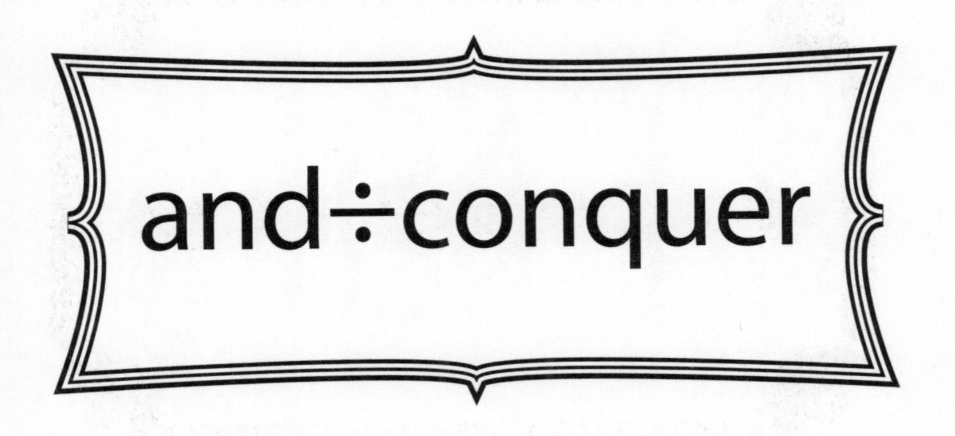

Answer to 48: six furlongs

Answer to 49: taking you out to lunch

Answer to 50: divide and conquer

Answer to 51: stretching the truth

Answer to 52: gross incompetence

Answer to 53: cryin' for more

Answer to 54: inflight movie

MEN MEN MEN MEN MEN

2

Answer to 55: mixed doubles in tennis

Answer to 56: coming up for air

Answer to 57: Two and a Half Men

Answer to 58: out of order vending machine

Answer to 59: rule with an iron fist

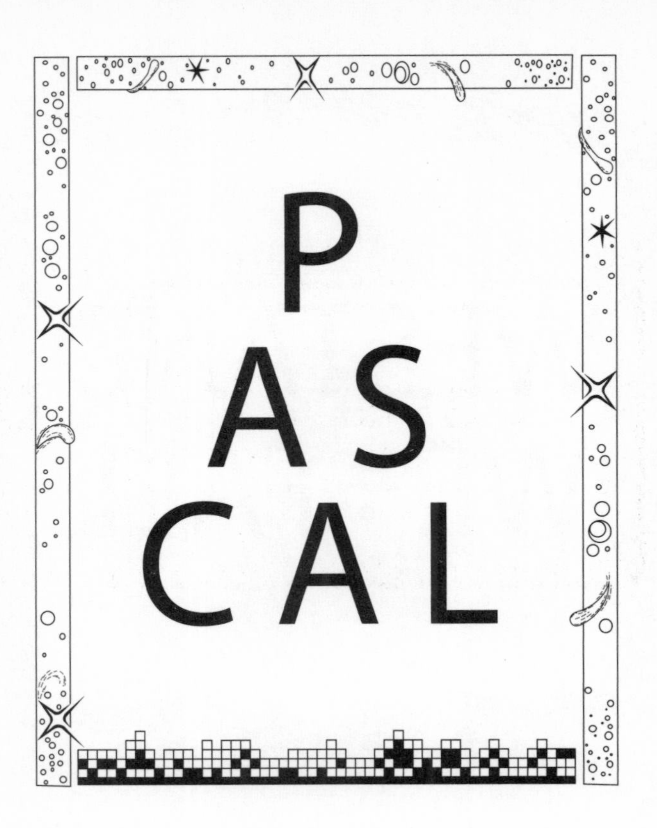

Answer to 60: won by a nose

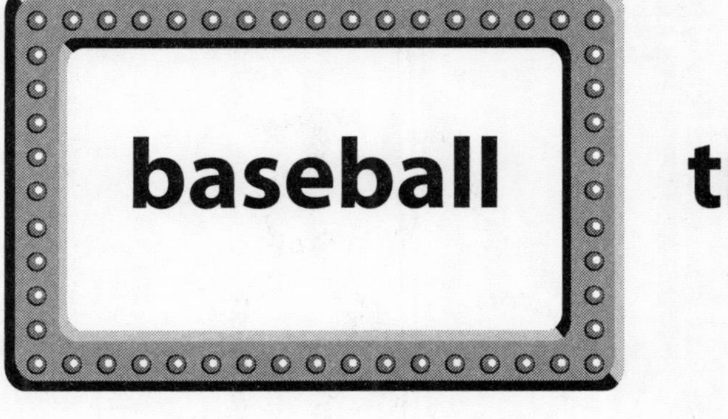

try

Answer to 61: united we stand, divided we fall

Answer to 62: Pascal's triangle

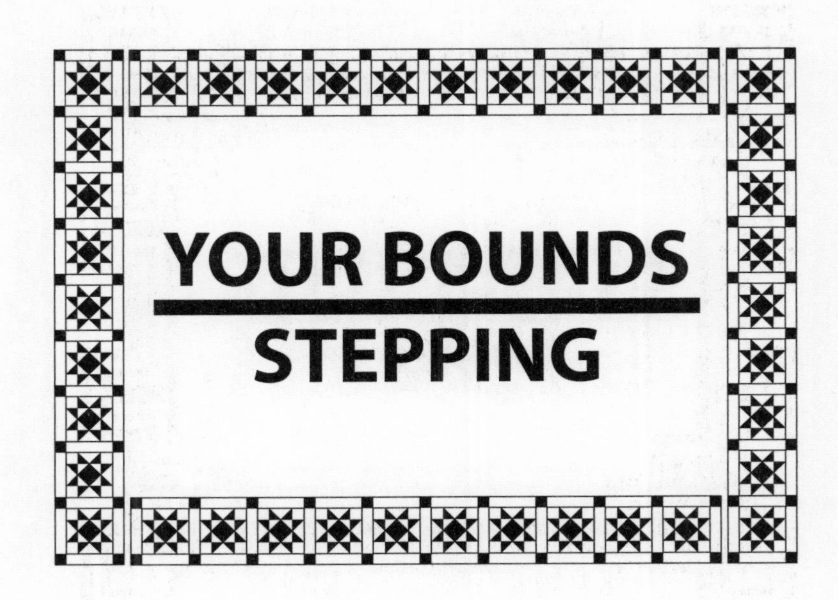

Answer to 63: baseball tryout

Answer to 64: backseat driver.

Answer to 65: overstepping your bounds

Answer to 66: gross understatement

Answer to 67: parting of the ways

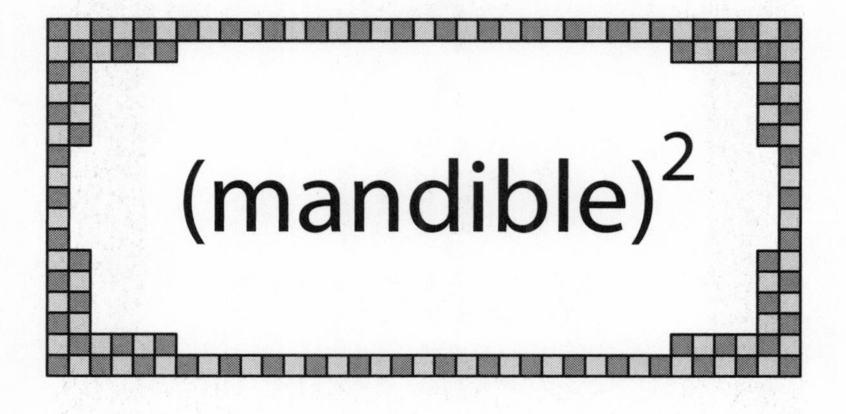

Answer to 68: the "Big Hurt" (Frank Thomas, pro baseball player)

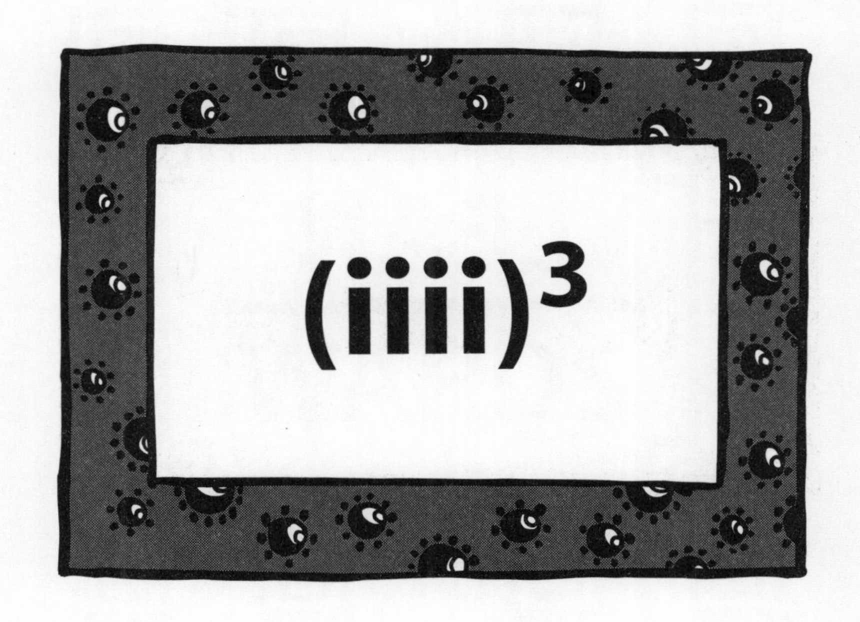

Answer to 69: paying through the nose

Answer to 70: square jaw

Answer to 71: ice cube

Answer to 72: lean over backwards

Answer to 73: the start of something big

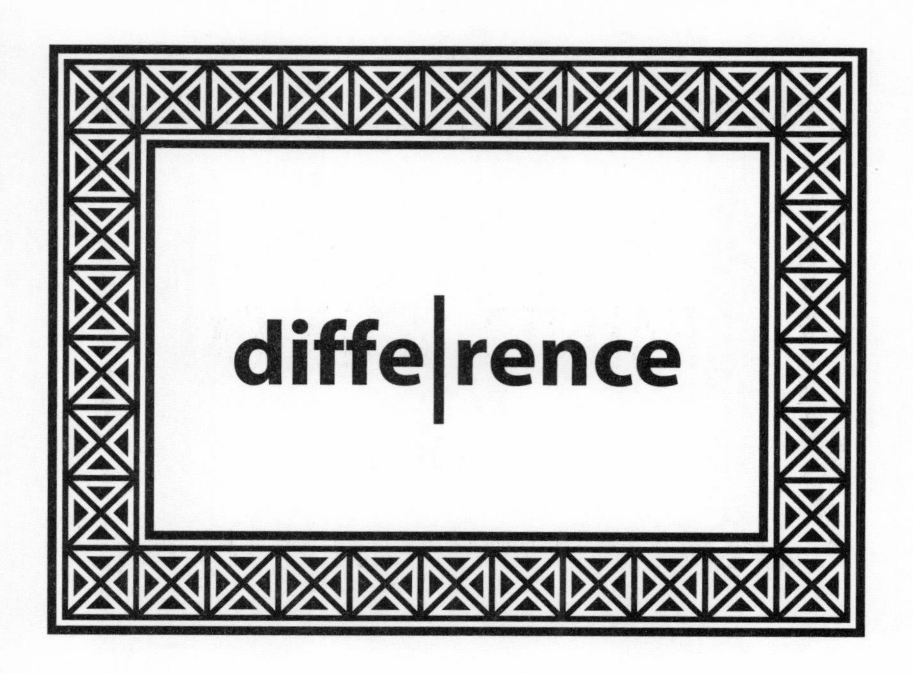

Answer to 74: American revolution

Answer to 75: it's the thought that counts

Answer to 76: split the difference

Answer to 77: not in your right mind

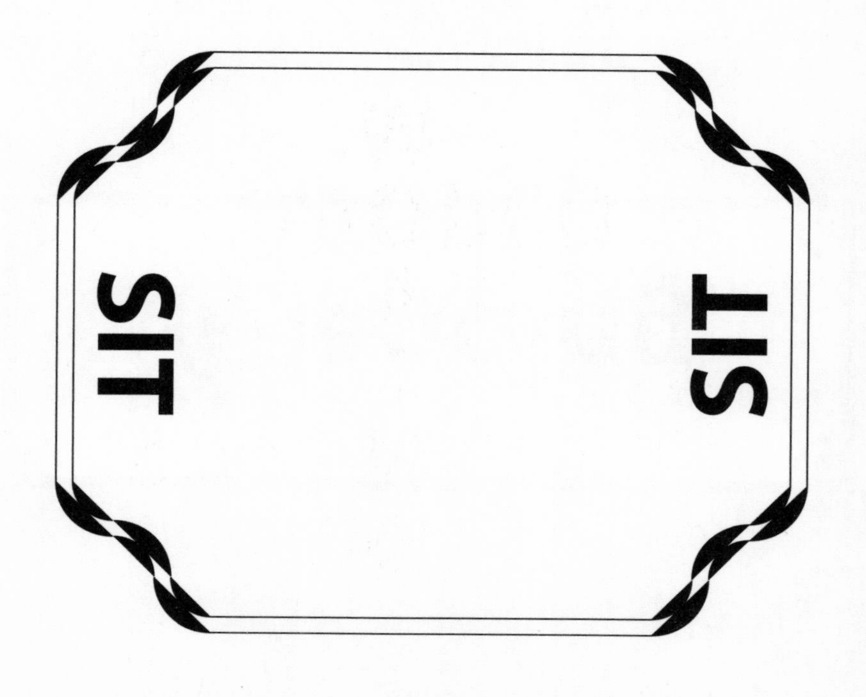
SIT
SIT

Answer to 79: circle for a landing

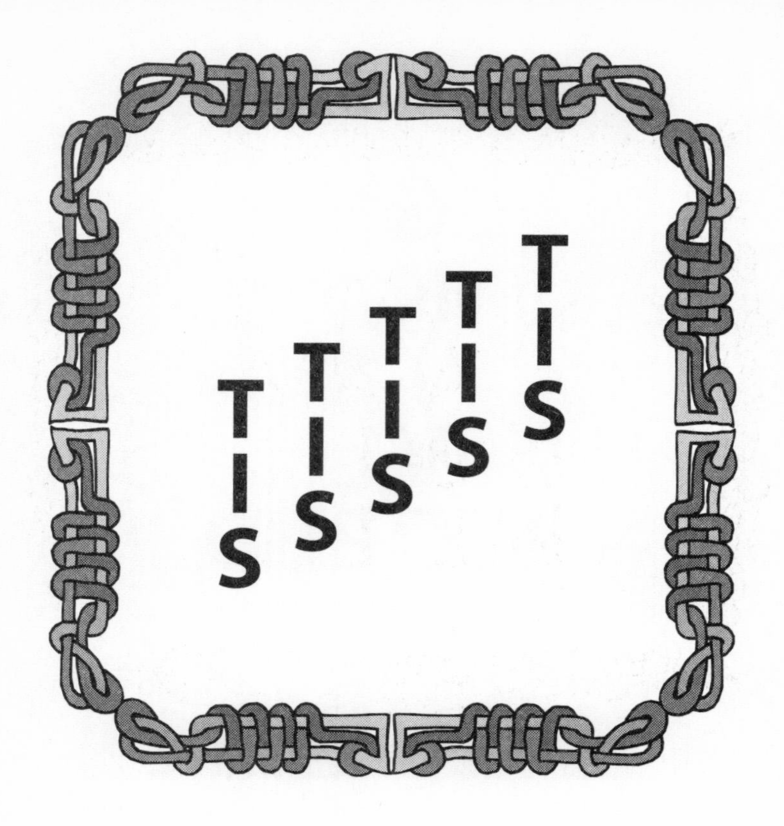

Answer to 80: sit on the sidelines

Answer to 81: moving up in the world

Answer to 82: sit-ups

Answer to 83: he's climbing the walls

Answer to 84: clear conscience

Answer to 85: scratch the surface

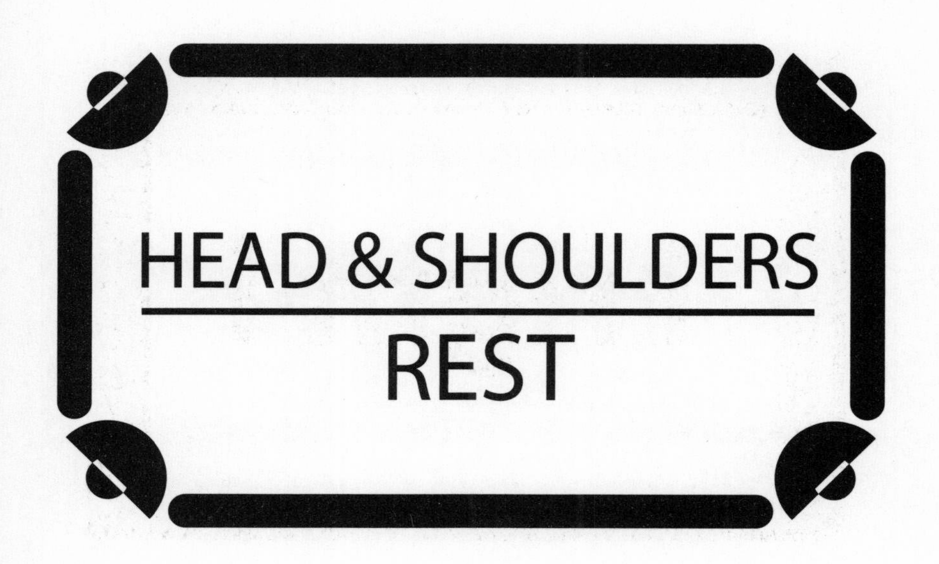

Answer to 86: for once in my life

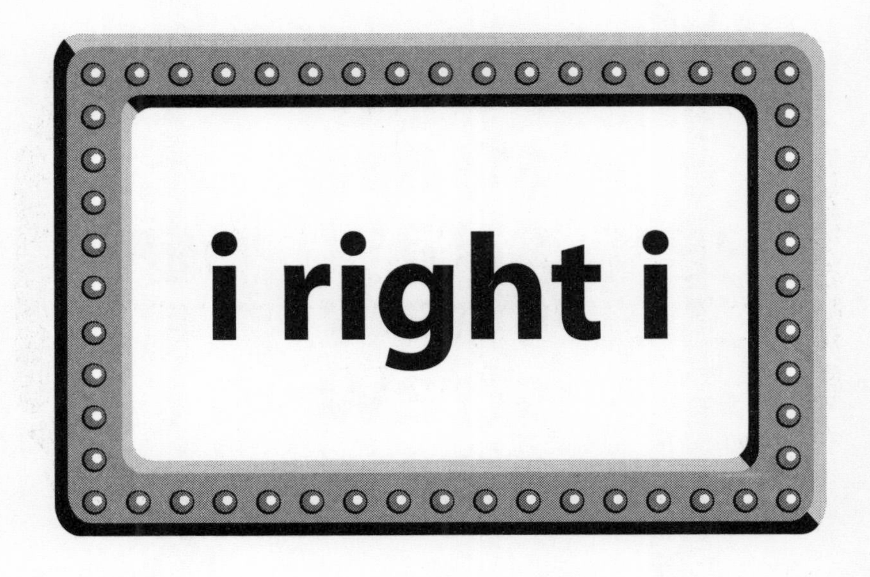

Answer to 87: wide awake

Answer to 88: head and shoulders above the rest

Answer to 89: right between the eyes

Answer to 90: this is the last straw

Answer to 91: you have come full circle

Answer to 92: tighten your belt

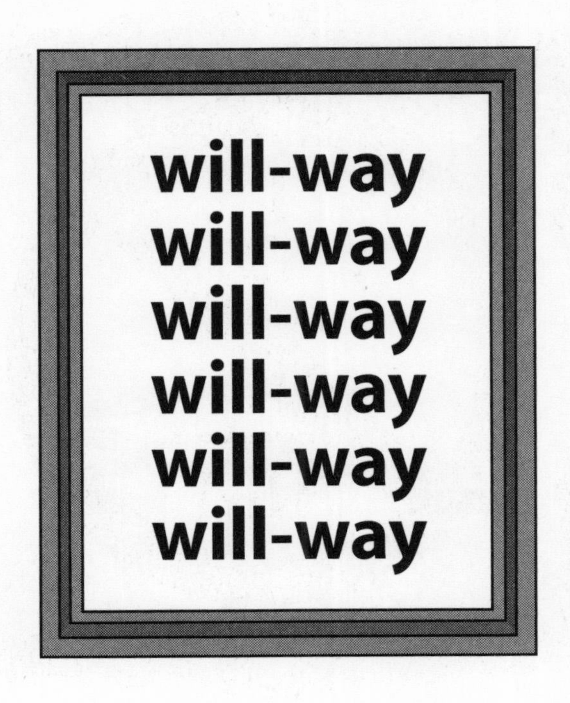

Answer to 93: it's for the best

Answer to 94: don't look down on him

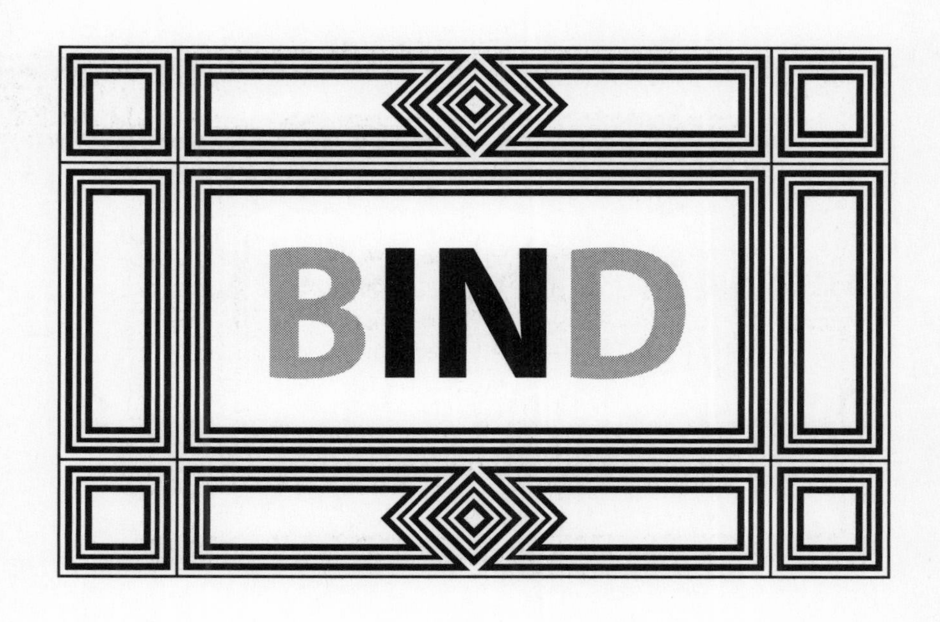

Answer to 95: where there's a will there's a way

Answer to 96: lay down the law

chance

Answer to 97: in a bind

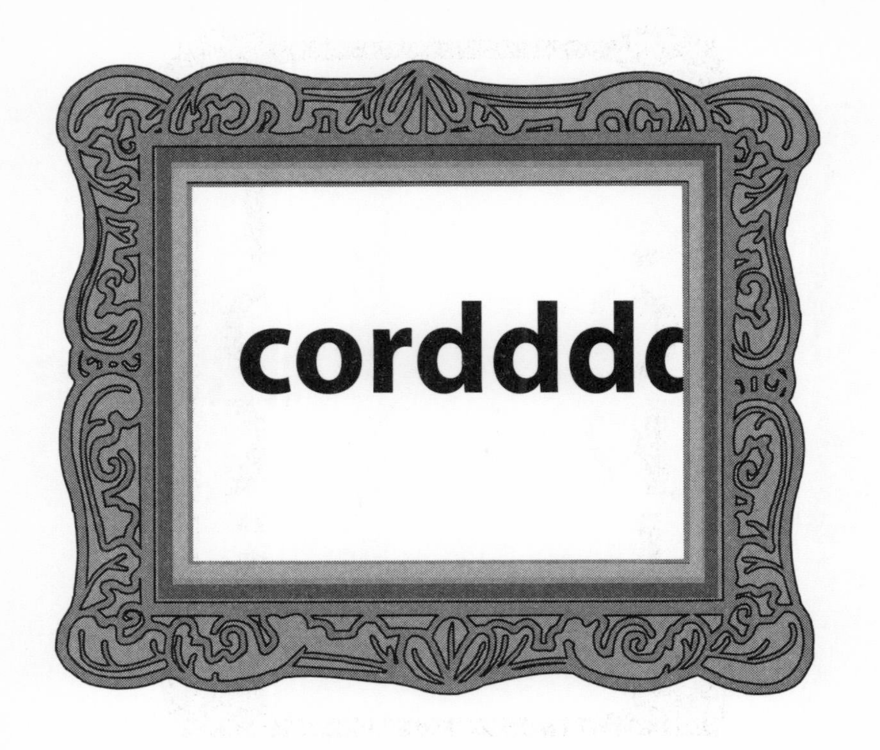

Answer to 98: you are one step ahead of me

Answer to 99: I have an outside chance

Answer to 100: extension cord

Answer to 101: side-splitting joke

Answer to 102: roll with the punches

Answer to 103: raise some eyebrows

Answer to 104: a pound of flesh

Answer to 105: Seattle, Washington

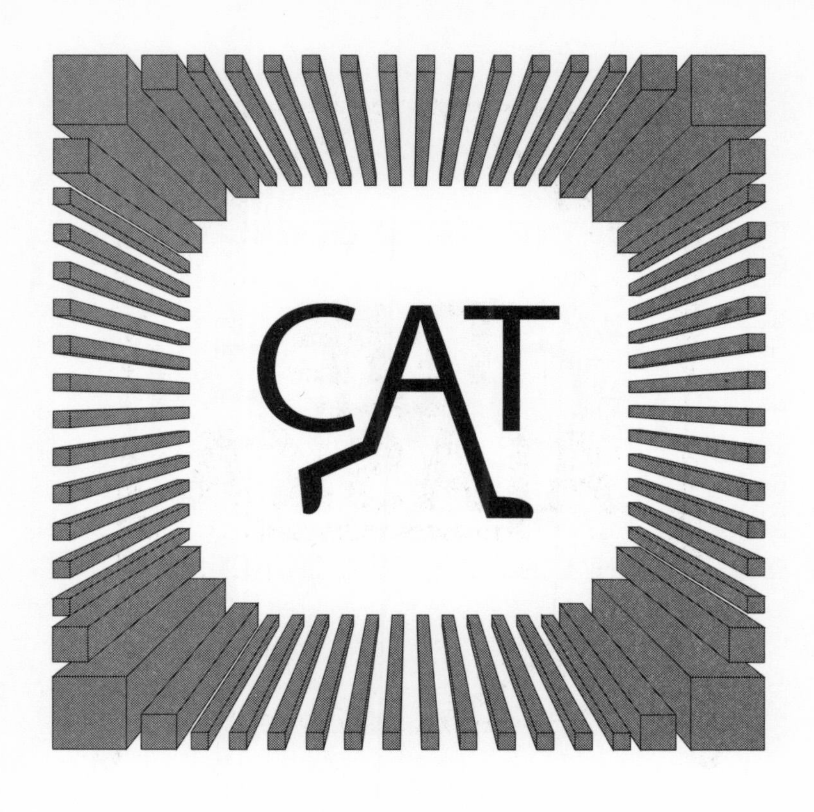

Answer to 106: go against the grain

Answer to 107: throw in the towel

Answer to 108: cat walk

Answer to 109: the Alaska Pipeline

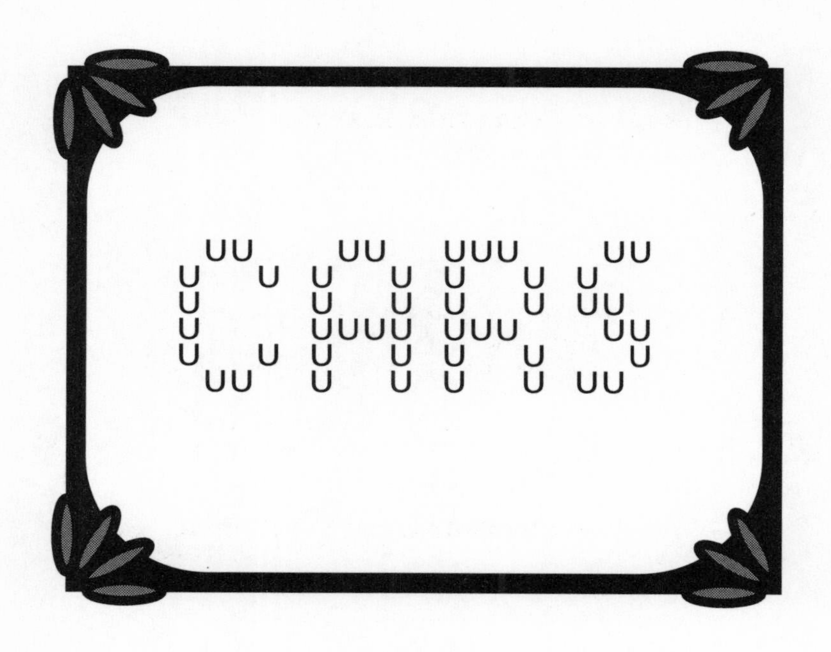

Answer to 110: *The Sun Also Rises*

Answer to 1.1.1: box scores

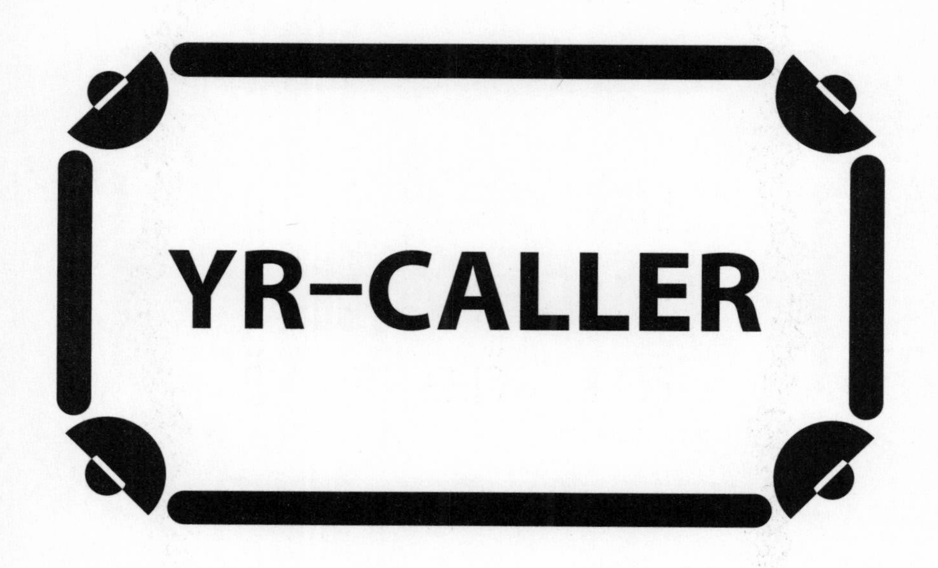

Answer to 112: used cars

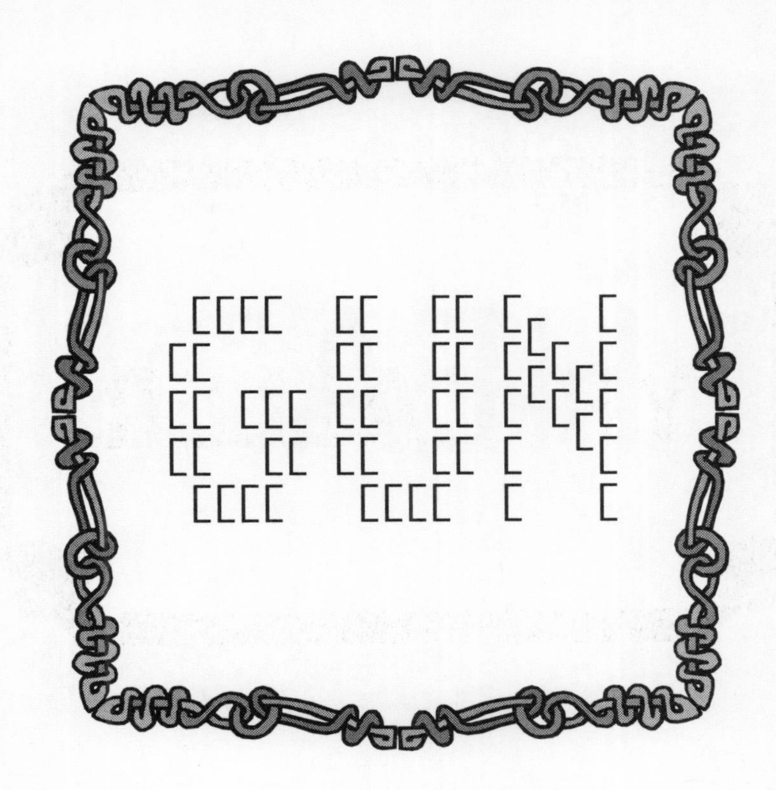

Answer to 113: writer's block

Answer to 114: wireless caller

Answer to 115: staple gun

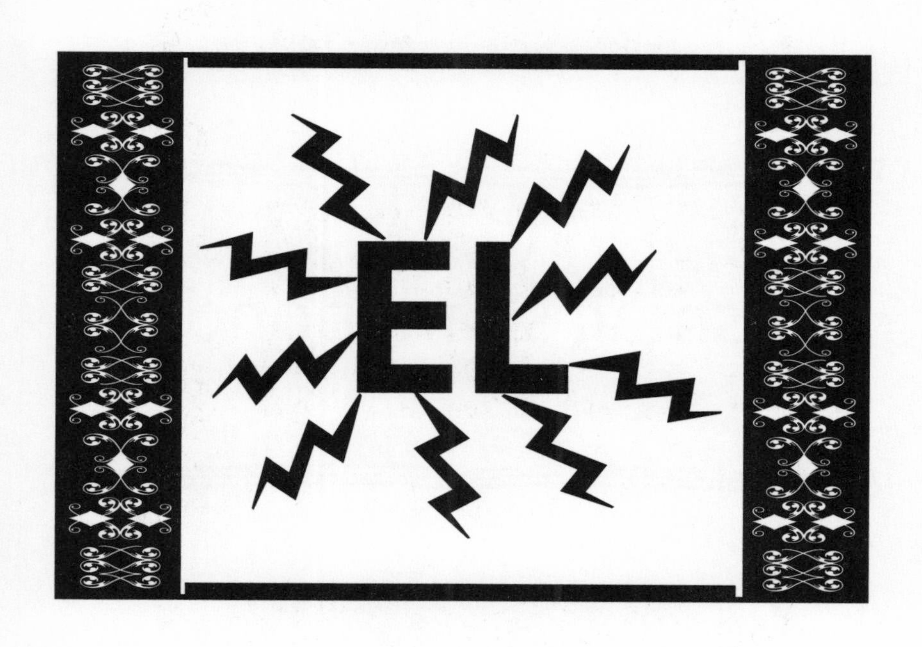

Answer to 116: eyes in the back of the head

Answer to 117: big fish in a small pond

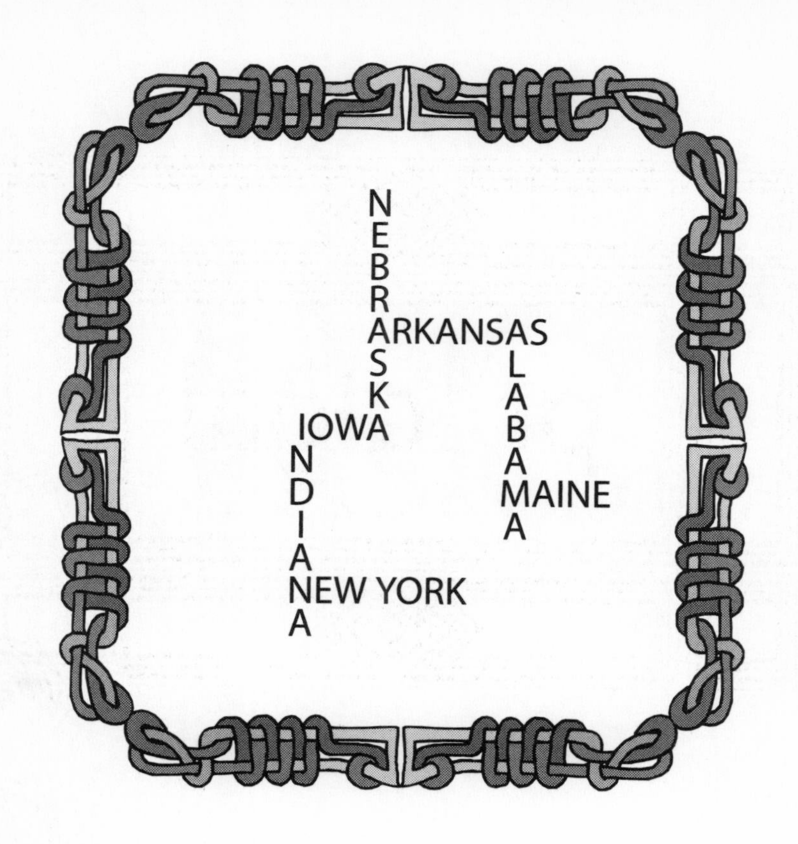

Answer to 118: electric eel

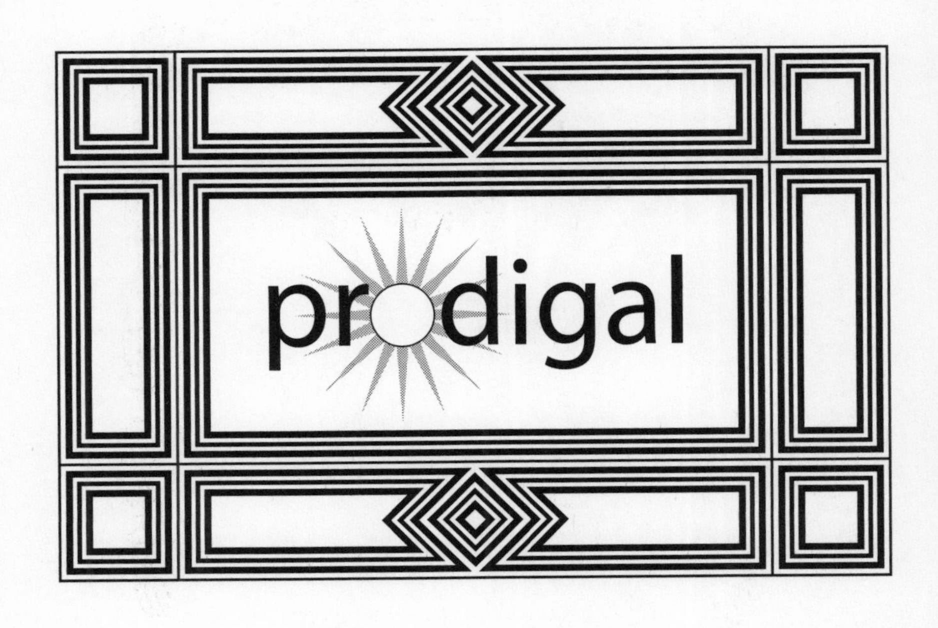

Answer to 119: back to basics

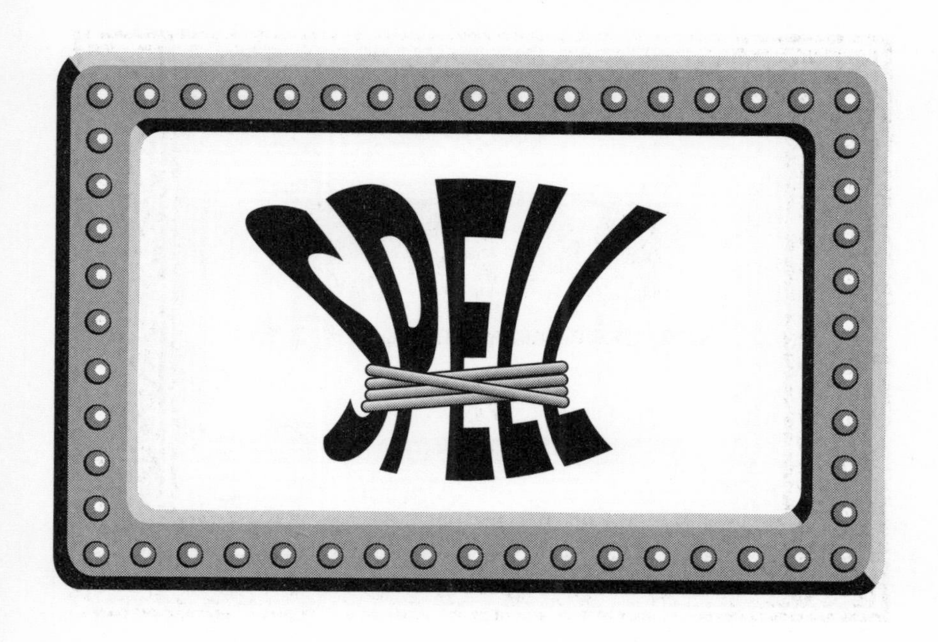

Answer to 120: United States

Answer to 121: prodigal son

TRANSLOSTLATION

Answer to 122: spellbound

Answer to 123: French quarter

Answer to 124: lost in translation

Answer to 125: get you wires crossed

Answer to 126: Farrah Fawcett

Answer to 127: suspended animation

Answer to 128: afraid of his own shadow

Answer to 129: eye of the needle

Answer to 130: etched in granite

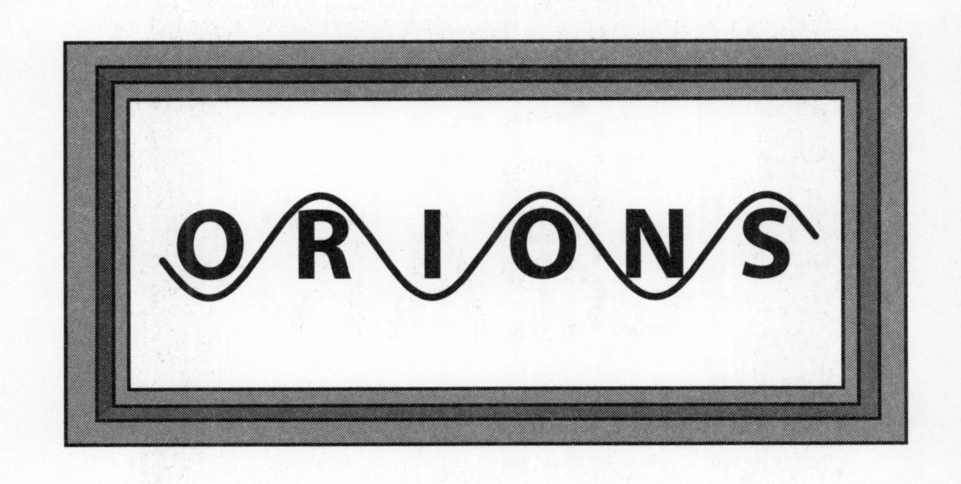

Answer to 131: round trip ticket

Answer to 132: spring a leak

Answer to 133: Orion's belt

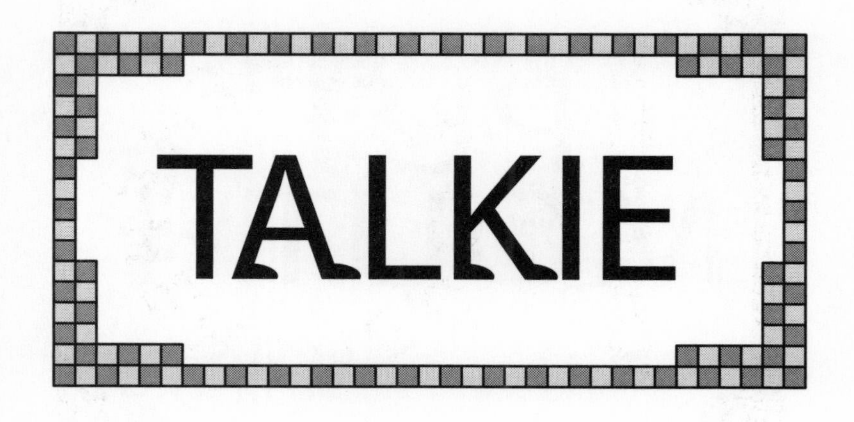

Answer to 134: mad dash for home

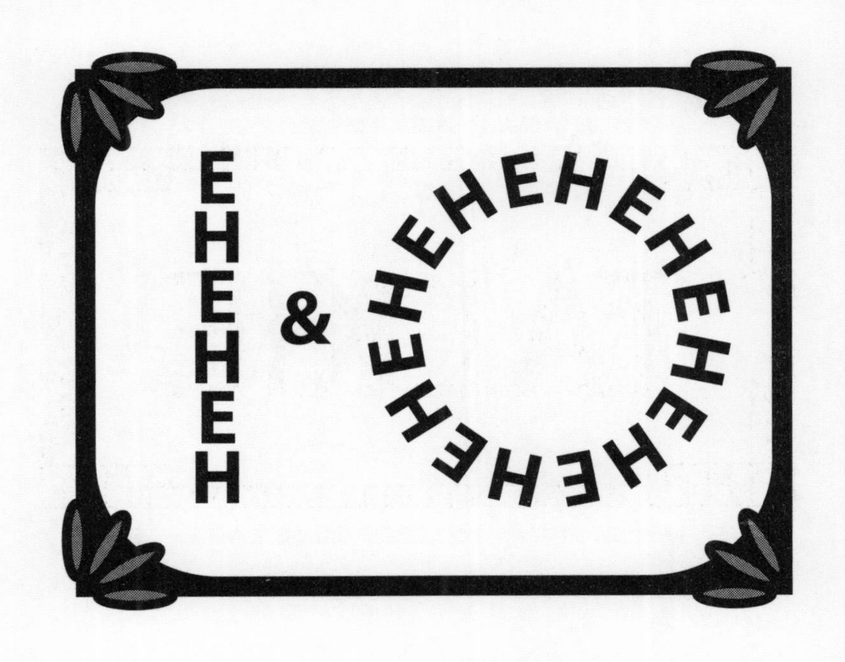

Answer to 135: put your foot in your mouth

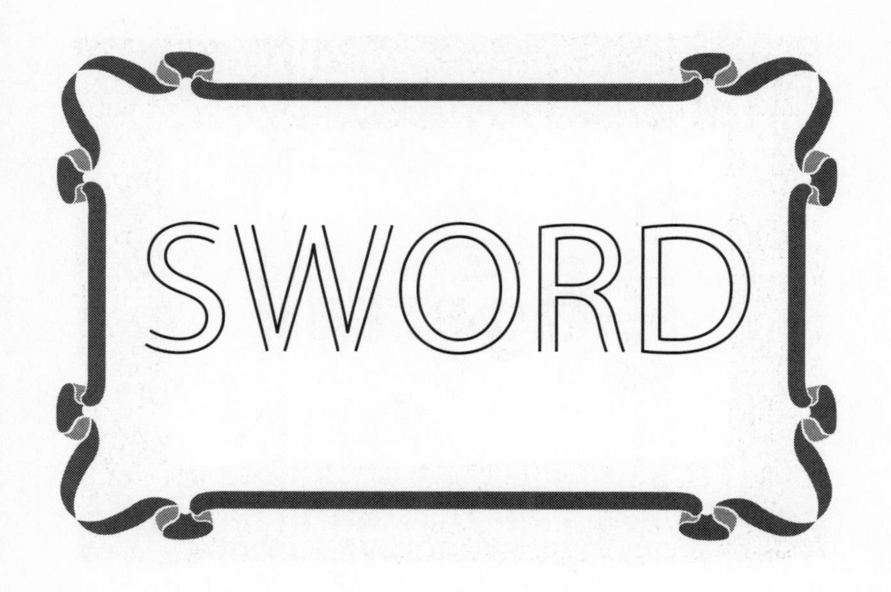

Answer to 136: walkie-talkie

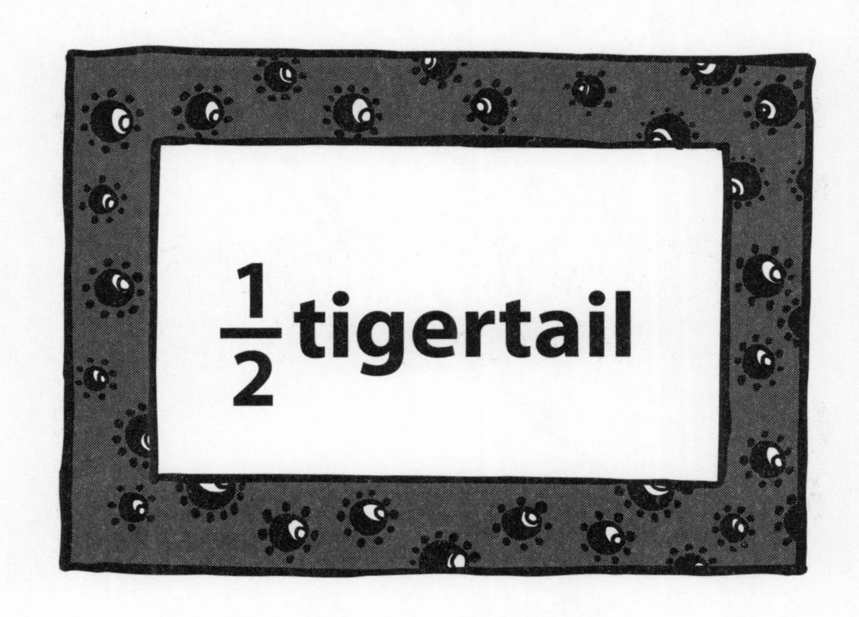

Answer to 137: he's up and around

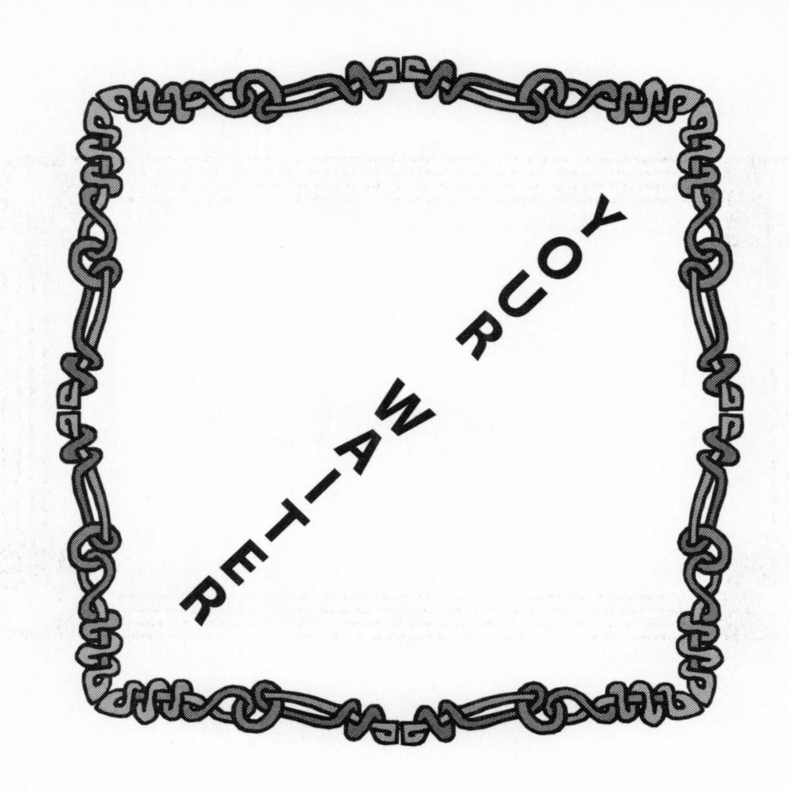

Answer to 138: double-edged sword

Answer to 139: have a tiger by the tail

Answer to 140: tip your waiter

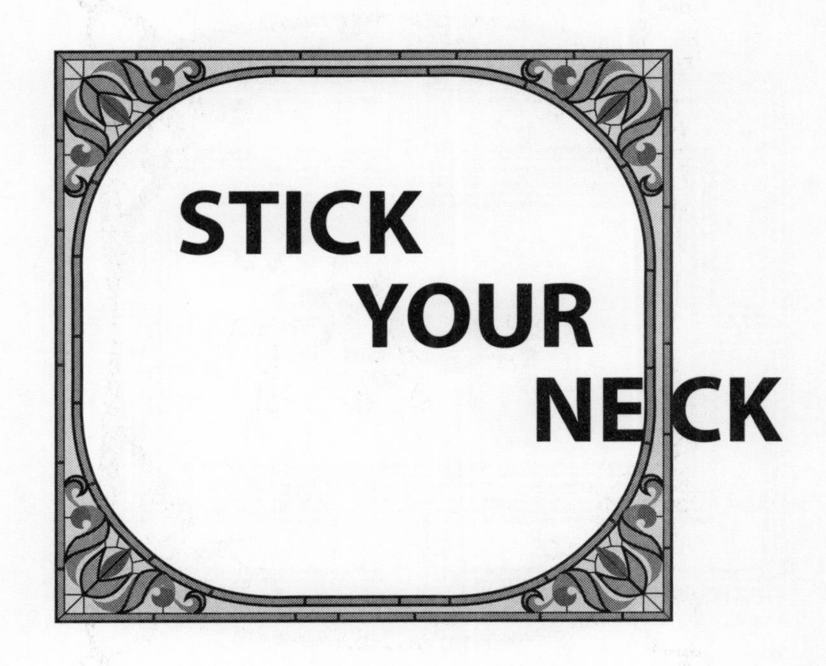

Answer to 141: straw poll

Answer to 142: pulling a rabbit out of a hat

Answer to 143: stick your neck out

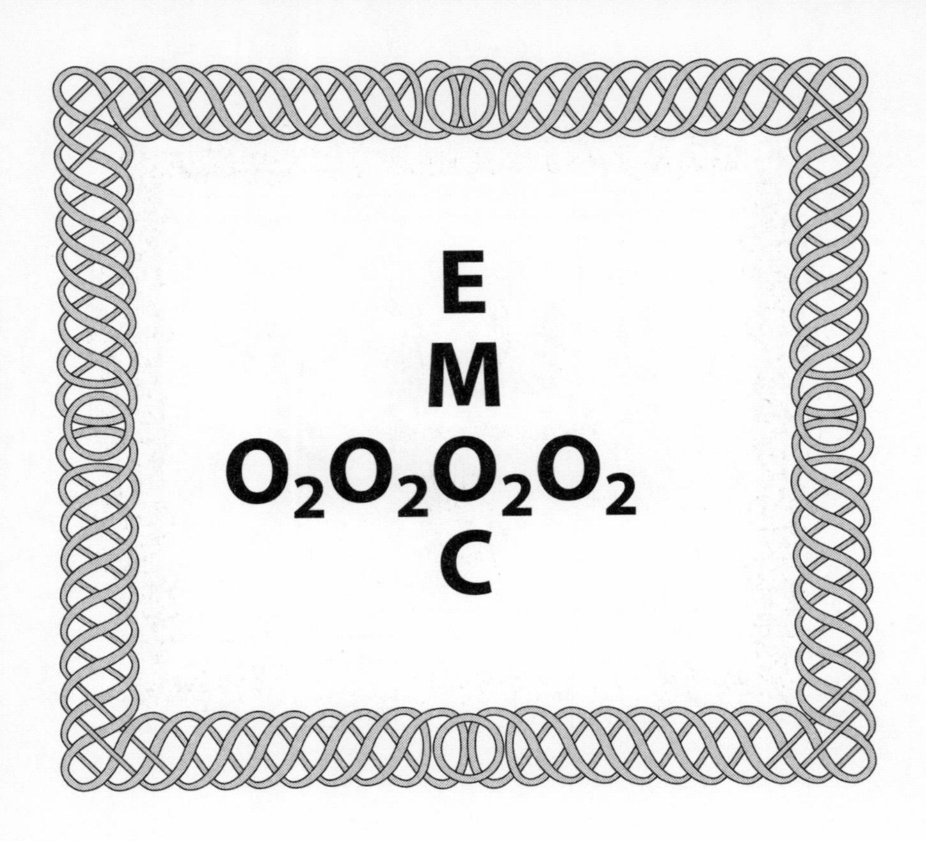

Answer to 144: snail's pace

Answer to 145: tie the knot

Answer to 146: come up for air

Answer to 147: split up over nothing

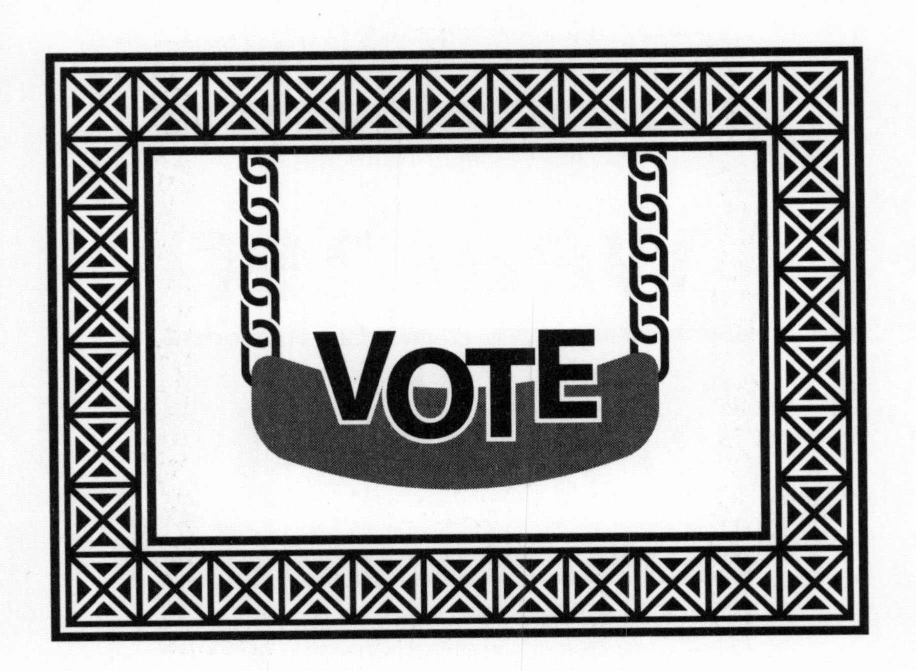

Answer to 148: three blind mice

Answer to 149: feeling under the weather

Answer to 150: swing vote

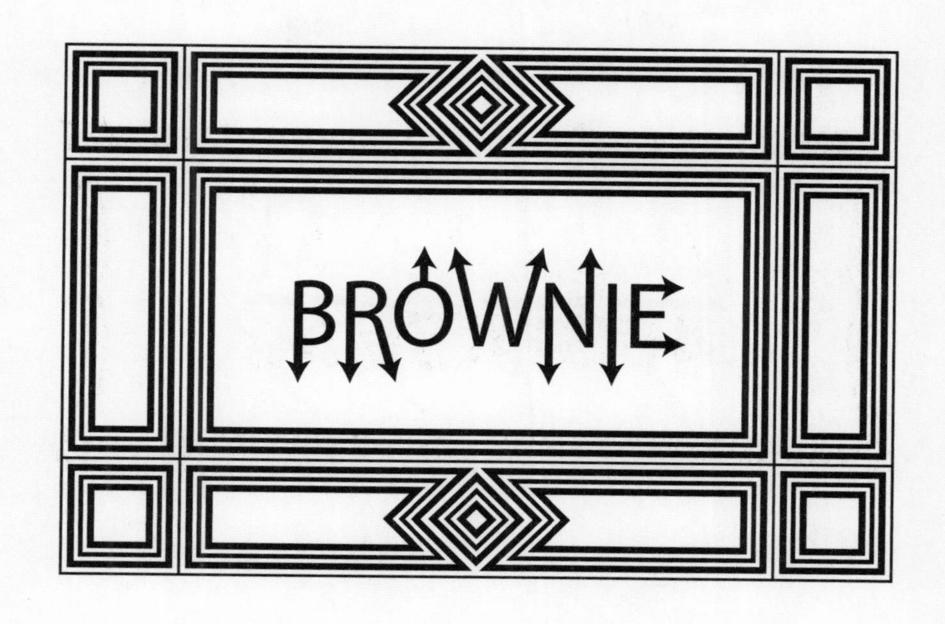

Answer to 151: hope springs eternal

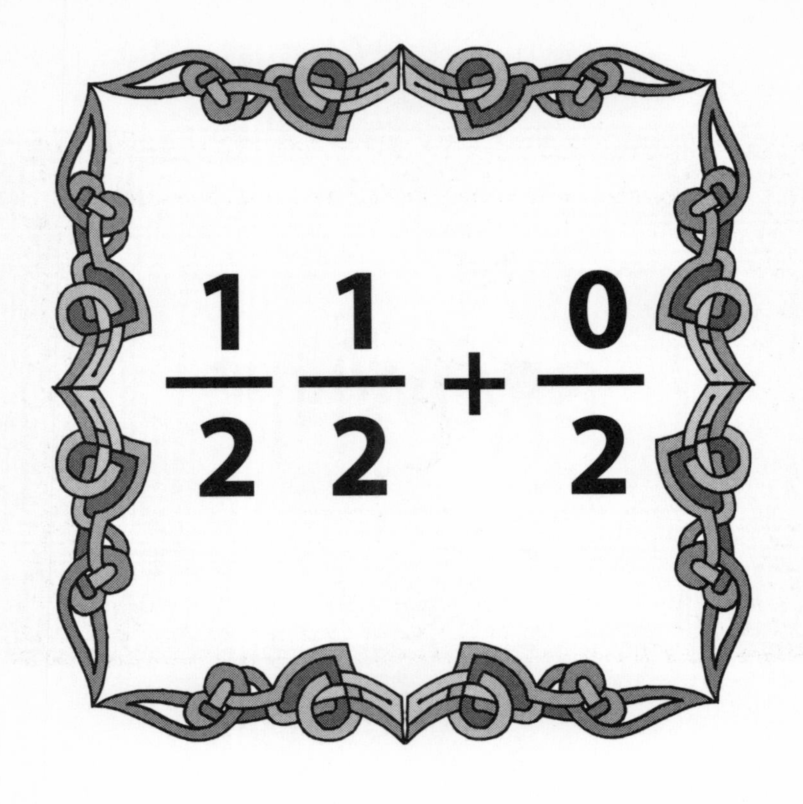

Answer to 152: different strokes for different folks

Answer to 153: Brownie points

Answer to 154: to have and have not

Answer to 155: salt of the earth

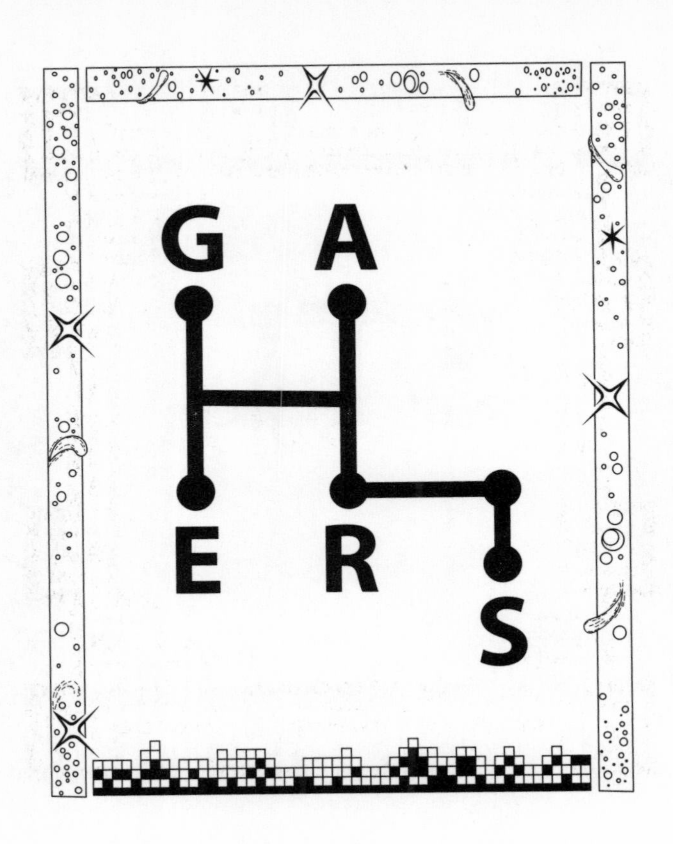

Answer to 156: deviled eggs

Answer to 157: short end of the stick

Answer to 158: shifting gears

Answer to 159: six of one, half a dozen of the other

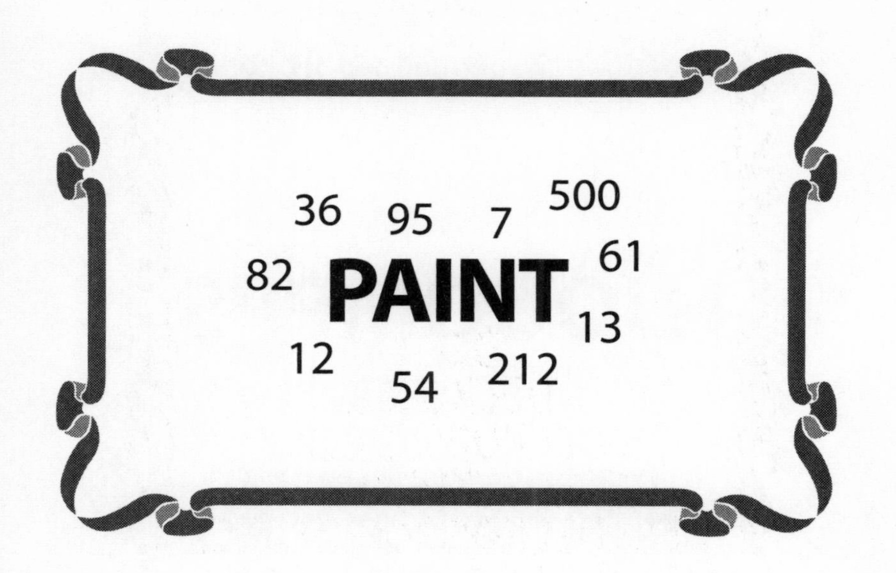

Answer to 160: spread the wealth

Answer to 161: jump through hoops

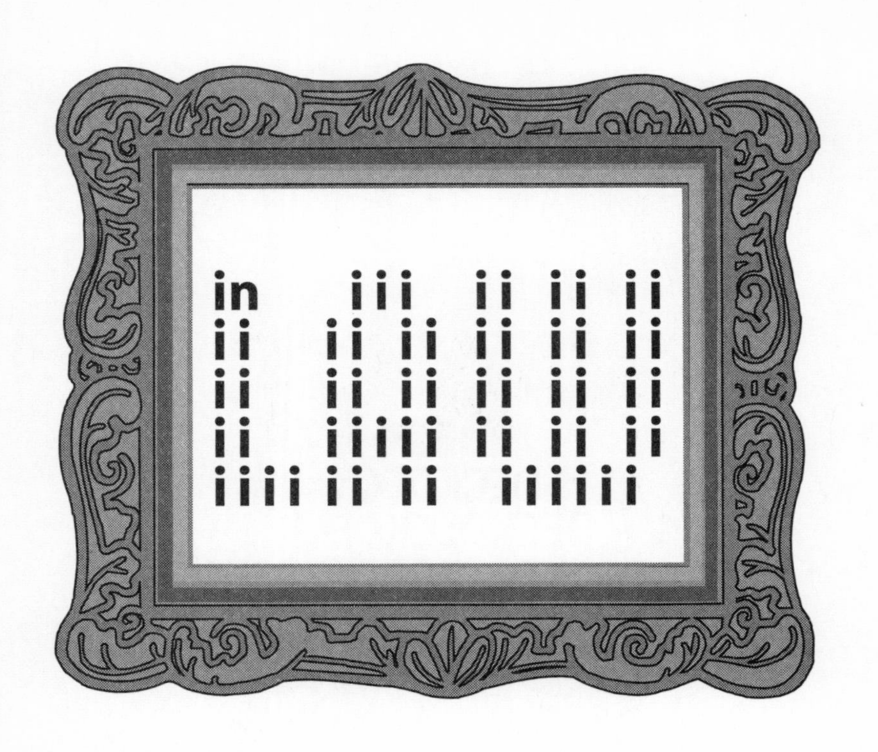

Answer to 162: paint by numbers

Answer to 163: stack the deck

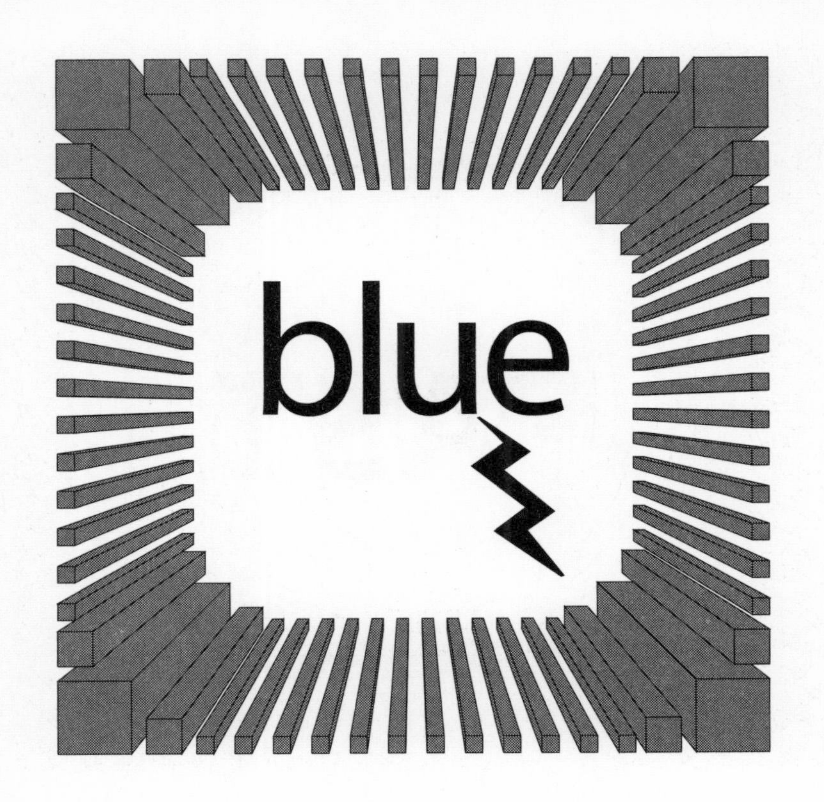

Answer to 164: in the eyes of the law

Answer to 165: erase the past

Answer to 166: bolt from the blue

Answer to 167: talk in circles

Answer to 168: zip code

Answer to 169: sales tax

Answer to 170: bite the bullet

Answer to 171: welcome with open arms

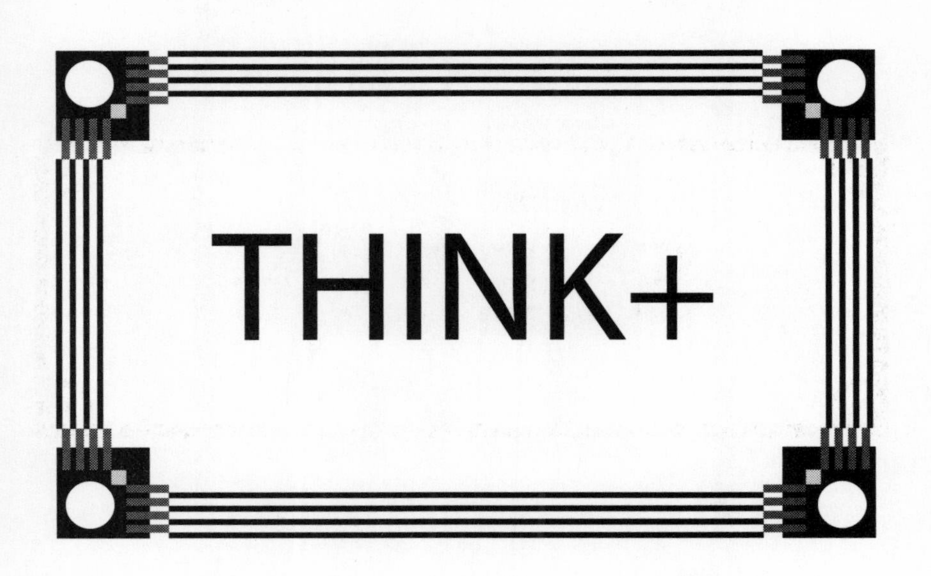

Answer to 172: going from bad to worse

Answer to 173: fair and square

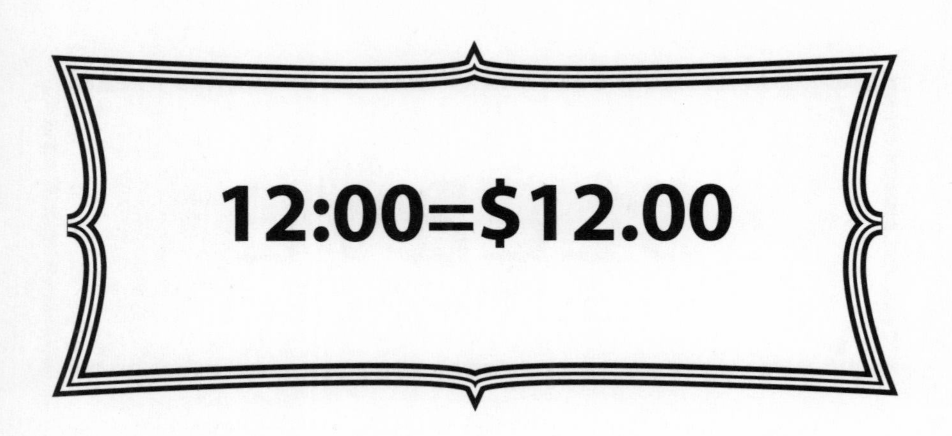

Answer to 174: think positive

Answer to 175: wear your heart on your sleeve

Answer to 176: time is money

Answer to 177: kick the habit

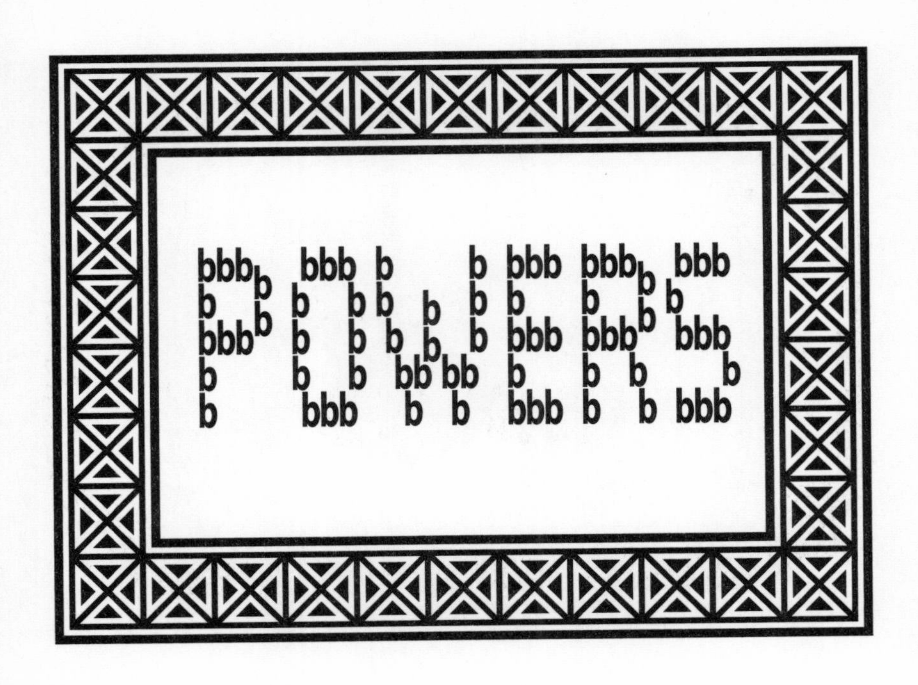

Answer to 178: go down in history

Answer to 179: turn up the heat

Answer to 180: the powers that be

Answer to 181: given to excess

Answer to 182: within reason

Answer to 183: plot twist

Answer to 184: vanishing point

Answer to 185: raising the bar

RINSERINSERINSERINSERINSE

Answer to 186: the back nine

Answer to 187: down to earth

Answer to 188: rinse cycle

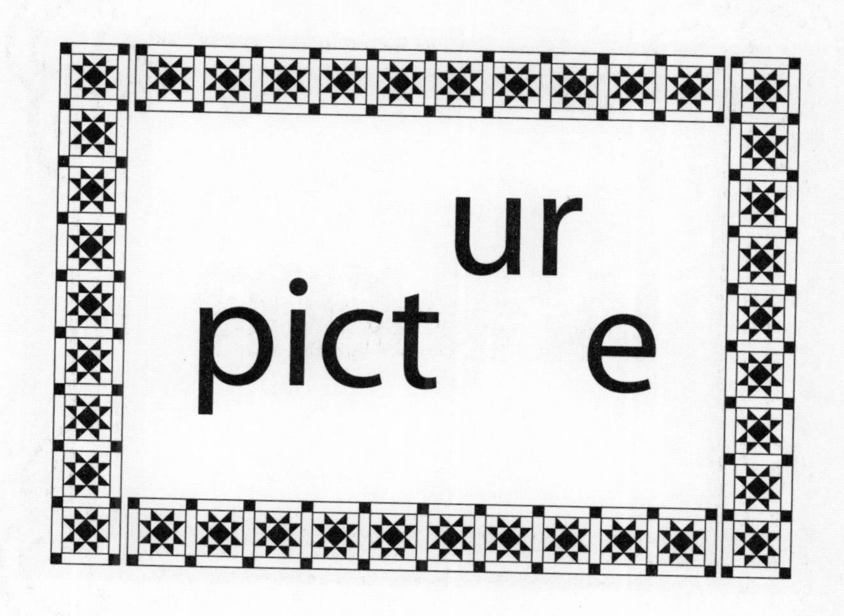

Answer to 189: circle of influence

Answer to 190: three penny opera

Answer to 191: you are out of the picture

loud

Answer to 192: worm hole

Answer to 193: bats in the belfry

Answer to 194: for cryin' out loud

Answer to 195: raise the ante

Answer to 196: put two and two together

Answer to 197: right on the money

Answer to 198: hopscotch

Answer to 199: downright awful

Answer to 200: bone of contention

Answer to 201: bulging at the seams

Answer to 202: forty winks

Answer to 203: pardon my French

About the Author

Terry Stickels is well known for his three internationally syndicated puzzle columns. His Frame Games column can be found in *USA Weekend* magazine, and is read by over 48 million people in 600 newspapers weekly. He also writes Stickelers (sic), a column syndicated daily by King Features, appearing in some of the largest newspapers in America such as the *New York Daily News, Chicago-Sun Times, and Seattle Post-Intelligencer*, to name a few. In Canada, Stickels is widely syndicated by the Metro News newspapers consortium. He has authored more than a dozen puzzle books, including most recently, *The Little Book of Bathroom Sudoku* and *The Little Book of Bathroom Kakuro* for Fair Winds Press. He currently lives in Fort Worth, Texas.

Answer to 204: *Men in Black*